Life Under the Sea
Stingrays

by Cari Meister

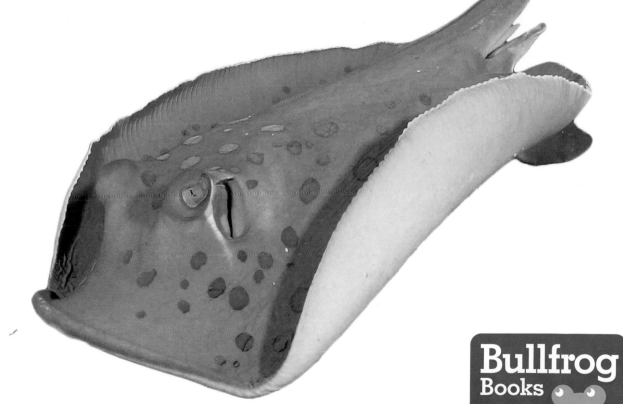

Bullfrog
Books

Ideas for Parents and Teachers

Bullfrog Books let children practice reading informational text at the earliest reading levels. Repetition, familiar words, and photo labels support early readers.

Before Reading
- Ask the child to think about ocean animals. Ask: What do you think a stingray is?
- Look at the picture glossary together. Read and discuss the words.

Read the Book
- "Walk" through the book and look at the photos. Let the child ask questions. Point out the photo labels.
- Read the book to the child, or have him or her read independently.

After Reading
- Prompt the child to think more. Ask: How is a stingray like other fish? How is it different?

Bullfrog Books are published by Jump!
5357 Penn Avenue South
Minneapolis, MN 55419
www.jumplibrary.com

Library of Congress Cataloging-in-Publication Data

Meister, Cari, author.
 Stingrays / by Cari Meister.
  pages cm. — (Life under the sea)
  Summary: "This photo-illustrated book for early readers tells about the physical features of stingrays and how they are adapted to live in the ocean. Includes picture glossary" — Provided by publisher.
  Audience: 5-8.
  Audience: Grade K to 3.
  Includes bibliographical references and index.
  ISBN 978-1-62031-102-8 (hardcover) —
  ISBN 978-1-62496-169-4 (ebook)
  1. Stingrays — Juvenile literature. I. Title.
 II. Series: Bullfrog books. Life under the sea.
 QL638.8.M45 2015
 597.3'5—dc23

                                    2013042380

Series Editor: Rebecca Glaser
Series Designer: Ellen Huber
Book Designer: Anna Peterson
Photo Researcher: Kurtis Kinneman

Photo Credits: All photos by Shutterstock except: Antonio Busiello / Robert Harding Picture Library / SuperStock, 18–19; Biosphoto / Superstock, 12–13; Dreamstime/Berndneeser, cover; iStock/shamino, 11; George Karbus Photogr / Cultura Limited / SuperStock, 16–17; Oceanwide Images, 12 Inset, 23tr

Printed in the United States of America at Corporate Graphics, in North Mankato, Minnesota.
3-2014
10 9 8 7 6 5 4 3 2 1

Table of Contents

Hiding in the Sand

A fish hides on the sea floor. What is it?

A stingray!

He has eyes on top
of his body.

They stick out.

He looks around.

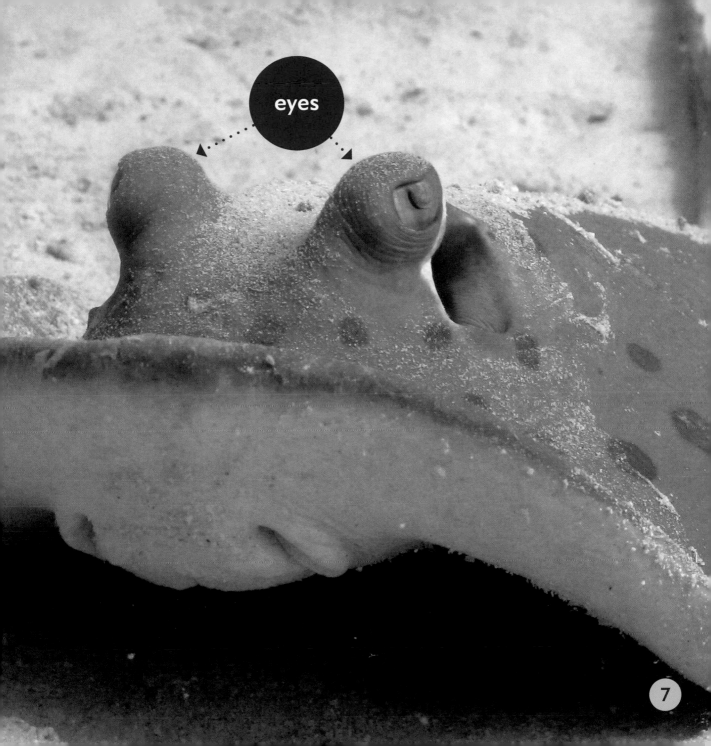

eyes

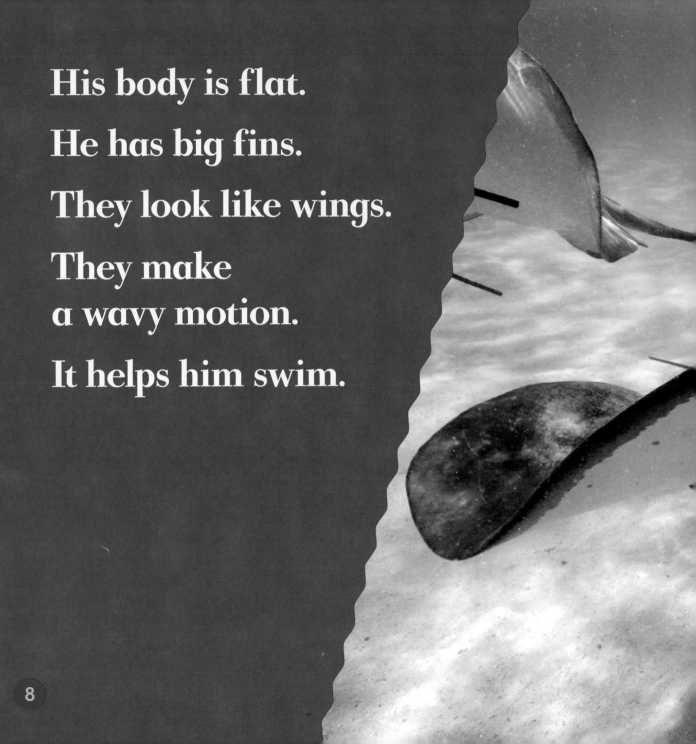

His body is flat.

He has big fins.

They look like wings.

They make
a wavy motion.

It helps him swim.

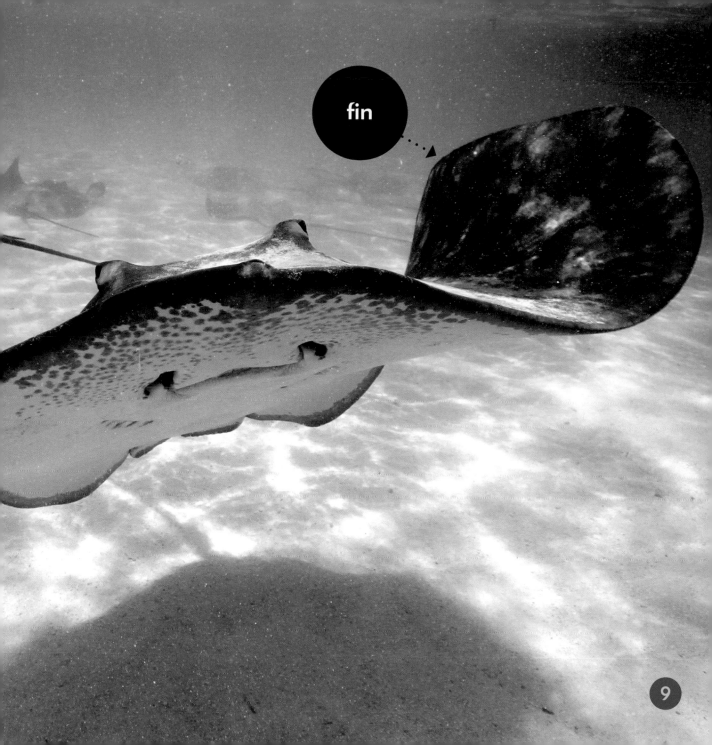

fin

Oh no!
A shark!

10

It's okay.

The stingray can fight.

His tail is long.

It has a sharp spine.

Pow!

The stingray jabs
the shark.

It swims away.

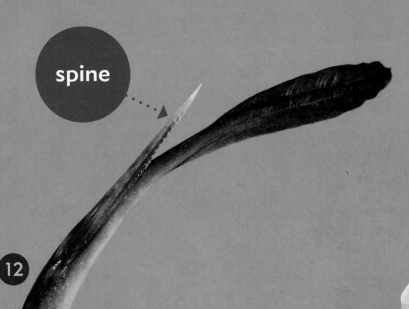

spine

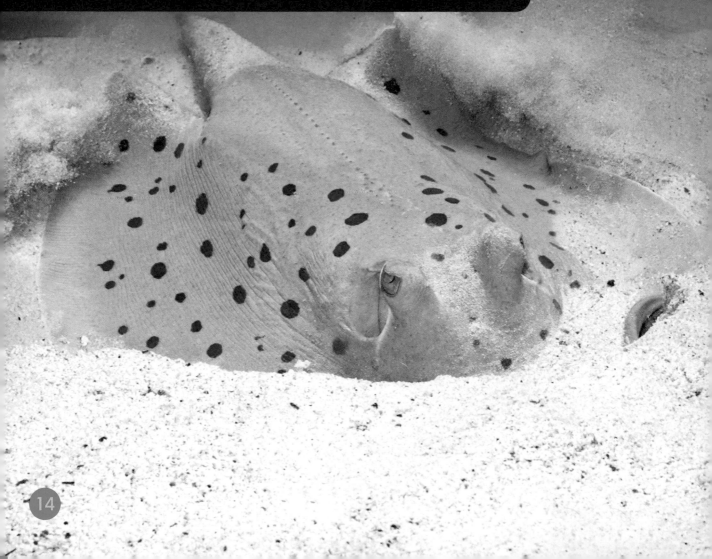

A stingray looks for food.
What's in the sand?

14

A clam!

She finds it.

Her mouth is under her body.

Munch. Munch.

She eats dinner.

Yum!

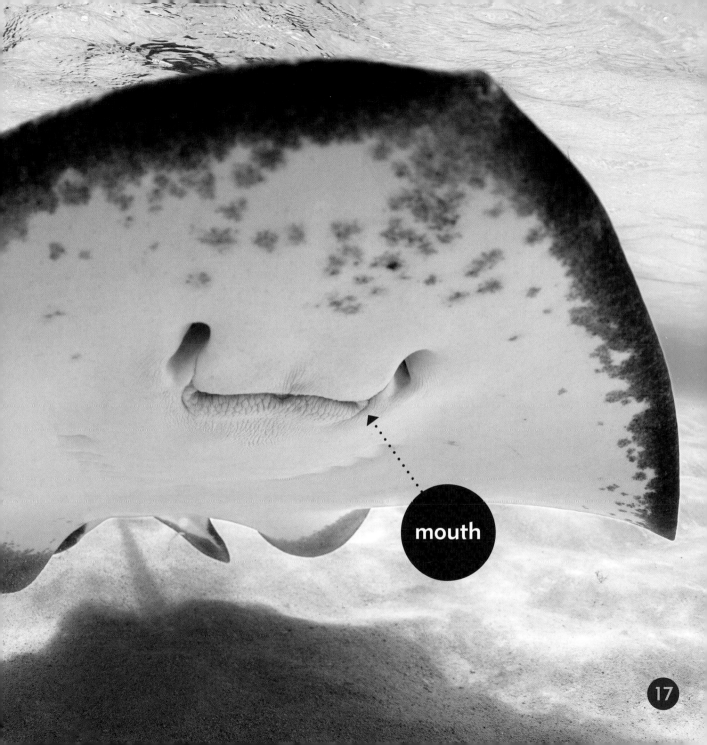

mouth

She rests.

The tide comes.

She rides the waves.

Look!

Off she goes!

Parts of a Stingray

eyes
A stingray's eyes are on top of its head.

tail
A stingray uses its long, skinny tail to defend itself.

mouth
A stingray's mouth is on the bottom of its body.

fins
A stingray's fins are shaped like a diamond around its head.

gills
A stingray breathes through gills on the bottom of its body.

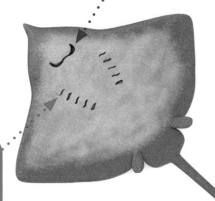

Picture Glossary

clam
A soft-bodied ocean animal that has two shells that open and close.

spine
A sharp point on a stingray's tail that shoots out poison.

sea floor
The bottom of the ocean.

tide
The daily change in sea level caused by the pull of the sun and moon on the earth.

Index

To Learn More

Learning more is as easy as 1, 2, 3.

1) Go to www.factsurfer.com

2) Enter "stingrays" into the search box.

3) Click the "Surf" button to see a list of websites.

With factsurfer.com, finding more information is just a click away.